Put Yourself Out There

# PUT YOURSELF OUT THERE

## 10 Mind-Hacks to Elevate Your Presence and Increase Your Influence

JANE ANDERSON

Cover design: Yna

Editing: Kristen Lowrey

Typeset, printed and bound in Australia by BookPOD

ISBN: 978-0-6480489-5-4

A catalogue record for this book is available from the National Library of Australia

# Acknowledgements

This book had been an idea on my ideas wall in my office for about four years whilst I grappled with it and tried to work out when to write it. Whilst I have written seven other books on the mechanics of putting yourself out there and business communication, I knew I had to write the book on what type of mindset it really takes to put yourself out there, at some stage.

The trigger for this book came after the year of the pandemic and 2020. That year the world truly changed, when we all suddenly went online, couldn't travel, we had to postpone our wedding and life as we knew it had changed forever. Entire industries have closed and many are rebuilding as I write this. Now really is the time to put yourself out there. Opportunities are endless if you're prepared to go out and chase them.

So, whilst a book cover has a title and the author's name on the front, it is a big team effort to pull something like this together, and there are a lot of people to thank. First of all, my family and new husband Mark. You support everything I do, put up with the endless hours of creating and working to support me in my passion. Thank you for tolerating me and doing all the thankless things that matter. Mum and Dad, thank you for teaching me how to put myself out there with grace, humility and service from a young age. Almost everything in this book and the work ethic I have has been a gift from you.

To my team who show up every day and help me to create projects like this book and keep putting myself out there. The only way I can do this is with your support so I am grateful to Sam, Katie, MC and Monique for implementing my crazy ideas and your commitment to helping me support others on their journey.

To the team that have helped pull this book together; I asked if I would be pushing the friendship if I needed to create it in less than a month and you all delivered. Sylvie Blair at Bookpod you are worth your weight in gold. Kristen Lowrey for your never-ending patience and sound-boarding support with ideas and editing. This book would not have been ready in time without your advice, work and guidance and working around the clock. I am beyond grateful to have you in my world.

To my mentors and mastermind crew; Keith Abraham, Rowdy McLean, Amanda Stevens and Andrew Griffiths. I'm so grateful for you all and the journey we are all on together. To Matt Church who inspired this book many moons ago. The legacy of your work lives on. Thank you for creating pink sheets so I have a home for all the stuff that goes on in my head!

Lastly, to my clients past, present and future. You inspire me every day and keep challenging me to solve problems. Thank you for trusting me with your careers and businesses. I'm so grateful to serve and to have found my passion supporting you.

Here's to you all having the courage to keep putting yourselves out there, too!

*Jane*

# Contents

Acknowledgements                                                    v

        Introduction                                               1

Chapter 1   Why Putting Yourself Out There Matters           5

Chapter 2   How to Build the Mindset of Putting
             Yourself Out There                              17

Chapter 3   The Four Derailers That Hold Us Back
             From Putting Ourselves Out There                27

Chapter 4   Mind-Hack #1 – Get Your Glasses On              33

Chapter 5   Mind-Hack #2 – Opportunities are
             Everywhere                                      39

Chapter 6   Mind-Hack #3 –  Crush Comparisonitis            47

Chapter 7   Mind-Hack #4 – Fly With Eagles                  55

Chapter 8   Mind-Hack #5 –  Celebrate Your Nos              59

Chapter 9   Mind-Hack #6 – Embrace Your Uniqueness          65

Chapter 10  Mind-Hack #7 – Be Vulnerably You                71

Chapter 11  Mind-Hack #8 –  It's Not All About You!          79

Chapter 12  Mind-Hack #9 – Get Comfortable
             with Discomfort                                 85

Chapter 13  Mind-Hack #10 – Be a Trailblazer                93

        In closing                                      105

        Endnotes                                        107

        Work with Jane                                  111

        Read more of Jane's work                        113

# Introduction

> "No-one knows what they are doing. You just have to put yourself out there and give it a try"
>
> **– Reese Witherspoon**

I was 15 years old and sitting in the car park of the shopping centre with my mother. I had gotten dressed after school into my nicest white blouse and black pants. Clutched in my hands was my resume and I was running through my head all the things that I had rehearsed to say. I remember the feeling of dread and the fear of rejection, as I was preparing to head into the shoe store to apply for my first casual job. It was the fear of putting myself out there.

All my friends were applying for jobs through ads in the paper but Mum had suggested I be more proactive and go where there was less competition. We thought about the best stores in town who seemed to have good training and were putting on school casuals. Mum and I had practiced answering the types of questions I could be asked and she kept reminding me to focus on what's in it for them.

I got out of the car and walked into the store and up to the counter. The manager whose name was June Maher was a lady in her 60s with a sweet, warm smile, glasses and short brown hair. She came to the counter and asked if she could help.

I said "Hi, my name is Jane Anderson and I'd like to apply for a casual role if you have any positions available".

Her eyes lit up and she said, "Oh that's wonderful. Yes, we are looking to take on a school casual. Do you have a resume?"

"Yes", I replied and handed it to her. It was quiet in the store at the time so she asked if I had time to have a quick chat. I said yes, so we went into the back and she sat me down. She asked me some questions, like what days I was looking for, how many hours I could work and why I wanted to apply for this specific store.

I told her that I'd had my school shoes fitted there since I was in kindergarten, and that I liked helping people and fashion. So, I thought I'd be a good fit.

She hired me on the spot and we agreed I'd do my first shift the following Thursday night. From that interview, I went on to work for the Mathers company, Sir Robert Mathers, his daughter Tracey Mathers and the family for 15 years. It formed the foundation of my career, even though I didn't know it at the time. It also taught me the most valuable lesson - that opportunities are everywhere, if we just have the courage to put ourselves out there. Since then every job I have applied for in my career (except for 1) came as a result of knowing what I wanted and putting myself out there.

In fact, most experts agree that around 70% of jobs are not advertised. And that means that 70% of opportunities are not advertised either

Today customers can be reached through social media or your own YouTube channel, and you can even self-publish your own book. The world has become noisier so the pressure to put ourselves out there to cut-through the noise is greater than ever.

I've spent the last 25 years helping people build their personal brands for their careers, as corporate leaders and as consultants. While there's been a lot of time spent on the mechanics of selling six-figure corporate programs, building websites and writing whitepapers, books, brochures, LinkedIn profiles and social media content, the real challenge has been getting through the mindset of putting yourself out there.

However, I have a confession to make. Putting myself out there is not something that I do naturally. I'm not a "centre of attention" type of person. I don't like being annoying or demanding. I'm an introvert and would much rather be behind the scenes and focussing on mentoring my clients. But I've had to learn to speak to over 100,000 people across four countries and 25 industries, to apply for jobs, create video content, write books, make phone calls and sell themselves among other things. It's taken a lot of mind-hacks to get the courage and overcome the fear myself, to be able to put myself out there and, ultimately, better help others.

*Put Yourself Out There* pulls together the top mind-hacks that I've used to overcome the fear and learn to put myself out there. My hope is that this book helps you to see that it is possible to apply these techniques and skills to put yourself out there, as well. I hope you can take away the knowledge that you don't have to have this ability naturally, and that you don't have to just have a gift of being comfortable with asking for what you want. You can apply these techniques, practice them and take your career, business and life to the next level.

I'd love to hear from you and how you go! Please email me with your stories to jane@jane-anderson.com.au.

Wishing you every success. I'm cheering you on!

Jane Anderson

# CHAPTER 1

# Why Putting Yourself Out There Matters

"It's very hard to put yourself out there,
it's very hard to be vulnerable, but those
people who do that are the dreamers,
the thinkers and the creators. They
are the magic people of the world."

**– Amy Poehler**

It was 2010 and I had just gone through a separation from my ex-husband, moved back to the city from my parents' place and achieved a new job. I was just starting to find my independence and had even started dating again. Everything was going OK.

And then things started to go downhill. I found myself in an abusive relationship, and I actually ended up in a situation where I had post-traumatic stress disorder from what was happening in that relationship. And it was really the lowest time in my life.

I began to have a fear of crowds, and I felt paranoid that something bad was going to happen all the time. I had recurring flashbacks and had lost all emotion. I lost empathy and sympathy, and I lost interest in everything else going on in the world. I was kind of like a walking corpse. I felt like I had no life, no energy. It felt like the lights were on but nobody was home.

My parents were very concerned, and I did try to look after myself and get myself back on track, but it just didn't seem to be working. I remember talking to my parents at one point and saying, "I just don't know that I'll ever get back. I don't know how I could ever put myself out there again to be able to get a job, to date, to do the things that I love to do. I don't know if I can even go shopping anymore."

It was as if I needed to wrap myself in bubble wrap, protecting myself from everyone and everything that could go wrong. I felt fragile and that I could easily break.

This episode of my life forced me to start really thinking about what it is to put yourself out there. I had already put myself back out there once - after my divorce, where I started again and had to rebuild my confidence and life from scratch. But then to lose that confidence again forced me to wonder if I could really do that again. Could I really put myself out there again?

I also started to think about the role of fear and how it takes over and impacts not just our mental health, but also our physical bodies in terms of our stress and sleep. And I started to think about what it was that I would have to do to come back from the worst time in my life. I had been so used to helping people, but I didn't know if I had the strength to do that again. But of course, ultimately, I did.

I want my story to inspire you to know that, regardless of where you are in your journey, you are capable of putting yourself out there. Whether you're currently quite comfortable with putting yourself out there and just want to get better at it, or maybe you're like I was and starting all over again. Maybe your confidence is really down and maybe you're trying to find your way back. But wherever you are on that scale, I hear you, I understand, and I've been there.

I've gone from trying to completely hide (emotionally and physically) right through to really finding my own way of being able to put myself out there. And, as I said earlier, this is not something that came naturally or easily to me at all. I'm naturally an introvert and I don't particularly enjoy putting myself out there at the best of times, let alone following on from an abusive relationship. I'm not a "centre of attention" person, but I love encouraging people and helping them find their confidence to do that as well.

## Putting Yourself Out There: What is it, and why does it matter?

There used to be a saying that "good things come to those who wait", but times have changed. The pace of change, the rise of social media, video, podcasting and creating your own platforms have meant our access to information and ability to get in front of the right people has exploded. There is now a level playing field. It's time to step up, stand out and put yourself out there.

But the reality is that only around 1% of people actually create online profiles, write content, share their ideas and chase what they want. You need to be part of that 1%.

*Putting Yourself Out There* is about marketing you and your business or career. It's about developing your reputation and consolidating your impressions so that you are showing the world what you want to be known for. In short, it's teaching you how to self-package your values for your audience. This is something that, as a personal branding expert, I've been helping people do for the last 25 years.

But why does it matter?

Trust inspires your employees and your community. Trust reassures your customers and clients. Trust also makes your business a success. Trust is perhaps more important today than it's ever been before. Today we're buying services and products from people we've never met, in locations we've never been to. Trust is what lets us have confidence in undertaking those transactions.

## Why We Don't Put Ourselves Out There

Nick Barnsdall is my good friend and co-founder of our business, the Business Ignite Project. He's also a business consultant, the author of *Better Business Better Life* and the founder of the Navig8biz Community. He runs webinars and online courses and hosts the *Better Business Podcast*. But 10 years ago he was a CEO with a strong aversion to personal branding.

You see, 10 years ago Nick would have laughed if you'd told him that someday he would be out in front of an audience, with a strong personal brand behind him. At the time he was highly reluctant to put himself out there, and he certainly didn't want to be in the spotlight. But he needed to get out and reach people. So, he wrote his first LinkedIn profile.

It worked and people liked him. They trusted him. He realised that through these channels he could build his audience, earn their trust and expand his influence. That meant that he was able to reach people, and speak to them about his business and opportunities. Since then Nick has built 34 companies, is the owner and director of 13 companies and his businesses generate over $100 million each year.

## We're Less Noisy Than People Think

People are often held back from really putting themselves out there for fear of being thought 'noisy' or 'annoying'. It is possible to be both of those things, but only if you aren't working from a place of authenticity with a focus on providing value to your community. If you don't engage authentically, you'll certainly disappear into that noise. Here's an example.

10 years ago when I first started writing copy for newsletters and websites and social media, I had one really big fear. My fear was the unsubscribe button. I would hold back from writing what I wanted to say, from the consistency of sending a newsletter every week, from posting  something on social

media every day because I had a fear of being annoying. I had a fear that I was being too noisy and that people perhaps wouldn't agree with what I would say. They don't want to engage with what I'm writing. They don't agree with me.

As a result, my writing became vanilla. It became watered down. I couldn't engage with anyone because I was trying to engage with everyone. The irony was that when I would send something, people did start unsubscribing because they had forgotten who I was.

Today I see people facing the same challenge. But when you give into the fear of being too noisy, you do yourself more harm than good. People then really will start unsubscribing simply because you have not created a memorable, engaging personal brand. If you're not adding value and they don't miss you, then why would they bother continuing to subscribe to your newsletter?

The reality is that we're less noisy than we think we are, and people are paying less attention than they really are.

## The Confidence Scale

When I first start working with clients, I typically find that they're somewhere along a sliding confidence scale when it comes to putting themselves out there. This sliding scale goes from the lowest level, a level one, or "actively hiding", all the way through to level five of, "putting yourself out there".

# Put Yourself Out There

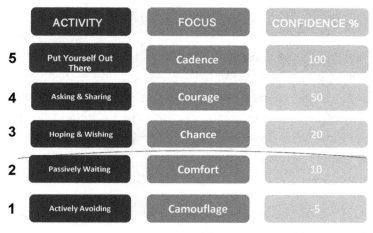

| | ACTIVITY | FOCUS | CONFIDENCE % |
|---|---|---|---|
| 5 | Put Yourself Out There | Cadence | 100 |
| 4 | Asking & Sharing | Courage | 50 |
| 3 | Hoping & Wishing | Chance | 20 |
| 2 | Passively Waiting | Comfort | 10 |
| 1 | Actively Avoiding | Camouflage | -5 |

© Jane Anderson

## *Level One - Actively Hiding*

If you're at level one, this is where you are actively trying to camouflage yourself. Your focus is to blend in and not be noticed. This may be okay for a little while. Maybe you just need to regain your energy. This is what happened to me. In my case I really needed to try and find my way to be able to get my energy back and overcome some of the traumas that I'd experienced.

So, it's OK for a little while, but you can't stay there forever. You've got to find a way to come out from hiding. When you're in hiding, your courage is obviously at the lowest it probably will ever be, and opportunities are not coming your way. To start moving out of this, the trick is to find your place and sense of safety and trust first. You don't have to push yourself, but you do have to ease back into your comfort zone.

## Level Two - Passively Waiting

Once you feel safe and secure, then you can start to move into what I call passively waiting. Passively waiting is this comfort zone. It's this space where you're just thinking, "Oh, well, I'm not going to use up too much energy. I'm not going to use up too much stress. I'm not going to put myself out there. Things will come along but I'm not going to try too hard. And in fact, I'm not even going to waste any mental bandwidth on it".

In terms of the courage that you've got, you're probably sitting at about 10% of what's possible for you when you're passively waiting. It's very low energy and that's OK for a short amount of time. But the problem is if you stay here then things aren't going to happen, or if they do, it will be at a very slow, haphazard pace. So if you want things to happen and change, then you have to level up.

## Level Three - Hoping and Wishing

The next level is what I like to call hoping and wishing. Hoping and wishing is kind of like the Dusty Springfield song, where you are hoping and wishing and praying and dreaming. In terms of putting yourself out there, this is where you're actively doing some things. They're still within your comfort zone, but you're giving yourself a chance and believing that there's a chance you'll succeed.

As an example, this would be like buying a lotto ticket. You're buying a ticket and you're giving yourself a chance, but you're not out there really trying that hard.

My good friend and mentor Keith Abraham says, "Hope is not a strategy". And when you sit in this area you may think you're putting yourself out there, but your actions don't substantiate that thinking. So, it's very unlikely that things will change while you're here.

Hoping and wishing can feel quite safe because on the one hand you're giving yourself a bit of a chance, but on the other you're not really that committed. You're not really trying that hard. It's a little bit half-assed.

## Level Four - Asking and Sharing

So, to really be able to start putting yourself out there, the next step is to shift from hoping and wishing to asking and sharing. Asking and sharing really means that you have a focus and a shift from chance to courage. This takes bravery. It takes courage to go out and ask for what you want. But the thing is you don't have to be doing it all the time. It's really just getting in and having a go.

Asking is not only asking what you want, but also how can you help? What can you do? It's also being generous and finding ways to share what it is that you can do or share what it is that you've got and how you can help people.

There's a real shift here from attention in to attention out. You're asking yourself, and those around you, "What can I do to serve?" My good friend and a client in our community, Renee Giarrusso, is a sales expert. I was lucky enough to interview her many years ago and during that interview I asked her, "What is the secret to being so good at selling?" She was and is an exceptional salesperson. She said, " In my mind I'm just sharing things. I'm just trying to help and see if what I'm sharing would be useful?" That conversation gave me a lot of confidence about how to improve my own sales with a focus on being able to help serve and share.

The trick at this level is to just have a go. You don't necessarily have to be doing it all the time, but you need to have the courage to just try it. Start by thinking about who you can help? Who do you need to get around you? What are the resources you need? For example, if you were applying for a job, you might need to get somebody to help you write your resume. And then you can have a tool to reach out and have a conversation with someone.

If you're doing this, then I reckon you're about 50% of the way there.

## *Putting Yourself Out there*

Once you've asked and shared once, then the trick is to repeat the asking and sharing, and the attention out, until it becomes a habit - or until it becomes part of your mindset. Doing it repeatedly is to have this mindset of putting yourself out there. And as a result, you elevate your influence.

When you repeat the asking and sharing, and the attention out, eventually it becomes cadence in your life. And suddenly you find that it's not uncomfortable or difficult, but just becomes part of who you naturally are now. So, while at the moment you might feel like, "I just don't have the ability to put myself out there", I'm here to tell you that *you do*. But how you do that, the next steps, just depends on where you are on the scale. And once you get that cadence you can practice the muscle of putting yourself out there and the courage to do that.

Putting yourself out there means finding ways of doing things that are uncomfortable and constantly exposing yourself to things you've never done before so that you become used to doing new things. Over time, it will start to feel so much more natural. Just as it has for me.

Putting yourself out there is incredibly important for all people in business, whether you're the CEO of a large corporation or a sole trader offering marketing services. It's the future of work. Similar to the future of community, thought leadership is equally important. Separately these two aspects of business can do amazing things for building trust and leading you on the path to success, but together, they're unstoppable. Together they bring you impact, influence and cut through, ensuring your success.

## 🗨 Key questions from here:

1. Where are you on the confidence scale?
2. How do you know?
3. Why do you want to put yourself out there?
4. What would change for you if you did?
5. What negative beliefs or stories do you hold about putting yourself out there?
6. How will you know it's working?
7. Who do you most admire of those who put themselves out there?
8. What does putting yourself out there look like for you?
9. What platforms might you use to put yourself out there (i.e., social media, etc.)?
10. When do you want to start?

# CHAPTER 2

# How to Build the Mindset of Putting Yourself Out There

*"The mind is everything. What you think you become."*

**– Buddha**

I recently got a call from a client, Amanda, who I have been working with. We've spent the last six months working on her dream business, her dream ideal clients and growing her revenue. She's written a fantastic book and we needed to shift her average sale from $5,000 to $150,000.

So, when she called, she was doing so to tell me she was referred to a very famous billionaire CEO who had requested a meeting with her. It turned out he had read her book and now decided he wanted her to rollout an initial program for some of his leaders. She designed the program and when it was priced we worked out that it would cost about $500,000. And this was just to get started. Through the computer screen in our meeting, I could see the sense of shock, overwhelm, disbelief and joy all at once. She said "I just can't believe this is happening!"

It turned out she had been delivering this exact same program in an organisation for over 20 years. But, she's just now at a stage where she can help others do it, which is so exciting for her.

So, what did she do differently?

Sure, we did everything like build the right collateral, LinkedIn profile, write the book and all the activities I've written in my previous books about how to build a personal brand. These are all the things that she did and you could see from the outside.

However, she really focused on putting herself out there.

It's one thing to know the journey that you're on and to identify where you are along this journey, but it's a very different thing to identify how to put yourself in a mindset of being able to put yourself out there. Once you have the mindset right, the focus is then on implementing and administration – the much easier bits. It's our own head game that holds us back!

## What's really going on...

You might remember back in your school days studying Maslow's Hierarchy of Needs. Maslow said that we need the following:

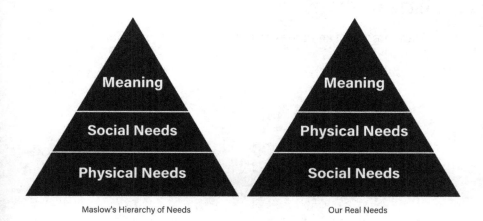

Maslow's Hierarchy of Needs        Our Real Needs

However, Mathew D. Lieberman, researcher and author of the book *Social*, has found that our social needs are actually what drive us over our physical needs. We have a basic, hard-wired need to connect and be part of a group of people. This is due to our "lizard brain" or natural instinct, which is our fight or flight and helps us to survive. So, in other words, we don't put ourselves out there because we're afraid we might actually die!

# Three Key Areas

There are three key areas to putting yourself out there.

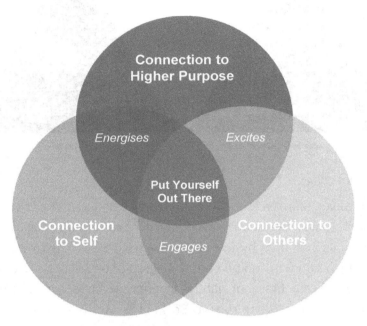

© Jane Anderson

## *Connection to a higher purpose*

At the highest level is having a higher purpose. You need to have a vision and you need to have something that will pull you towards that vision to help you get through the days when you find it hard or uncomfortable. Richard Branson said, *"When you have a vision, the vision pulls you."* I've found that to be very true.

Knowing others who have a strong vision and high sense of purpose will help you to create a common ground as it generates the fuel for a shared future.

## Connecting with yourself

The connection with yourself is the act of getting a strong sense of your identity. That means determining who you are and your purpose, but also what you're trying to achieve.

What are your specific goals and how do they align with why you are here on this planet? You want to consider the difference you are here to make and the mindset that you are here to serve and help, as opposed to it just being about yourself. To have a strong connection with yourself you need to understand your values, get the right people around you, get a strong sense of your own identity and find that feeling of abundance.

## Connecting with others

The second part is finding the connection with others. This connection with others is how you communicate yourself to others in a way that's meaningful to other people and doesn't make you sound like a self-centered narcissist. You certainly don't want to come across as being only concerned about yourself and achieving your own results at the expense of caring for anybody else.

Zig Ziglar said *"The only way you'll ever get what you want is if you help other people get what they want"*. So, to put yourself out there, you really need to think about how you can connect and serve and help other people and remember that it's not just about you. Because if it's all about you, people are much less likely to help you get there.

## Builds Energy

Once you can integrate your vision and your communications, you'll find that you get an energy within yourself. And that energy will help inspire you to find a way to make your goals happen. Suddenly you'll find that you're getting up early, working through the night, staying up late, travelling and even doing uncomfortable things. You find the energy to make them happen.

## Creates Excitement

When you've got that intersection of higher purpose and connection with others, it creates an excitement for other people. They love to see you achieve. They feel inspired and invigorated by seeing you really going out there and striving for your goals. They think, "Wow, this is amazing. Here's somebody who's really going for it and really having a go". And that's exciting.

It doesn't end there. Imagine that you've received an inquiry from someone who wants to come to work for you. And that person says, "My higher purpose is about working for an organisation like yours. Here's what I could do to help you". That would be very exciting for you, and in the real world that excites CEOs and HR managers. They know that hardly anyone does that. They hardly ever really put themselves out there. They just always apply through the recruitment process.

And because your approach and energy interests them and excites them you're far more likely to get what you want.

## Enlivens Engagement

It's one thing to incite excitement, but it's a very different thing to take that excitement and leverage it into action. In other words, it's much more difficult to get people to do *something*. In order to get to that step, you need people to feel like they connect with you. If you can get that connection between yourself and others, you will create engagement and that is where you're going to build traction. This is the space where you'll suddenly find that you can have conversations with people about what the next steps are.

So, what do you do next? Do you have a meeting? Do you need to go and speak to a specific person? Do you need an introduction? Do you need to get help putting your blog together? Do you need to do your podcast? Do you need to do a video? It's really up to you. But you need to determine what communication you need to do to make that connection with someone else happen. Because it's only through that connection that they can see your higher purpose and see that it aligns with their higher purpose. Once you've inspired them, you're far more likely to influence them to help you to achieve your goals.

Many years ago, I decided I wanted to work for a weight loss company. I was really inspired by the CEO's vision to help people live healthier lives, lose weight and feel better about themselves and overcome type II diabetes. I had the opportunity to meet him at a local chemist in our area. I knew the program well as I'd lost about 15 kilos on it myself. I loved helping people and had been heavily involved in corporate health and wellbeing programs in government as a Human Resources Officer. So, I decided to go along to the "meet and greet".

I introduced myself to him, explained I'd been on the program and my background. I asked him if I might be able to make a time to meet with him and share my thoughts on how they could deliver a great corporate wellness program. He was surprised and thrilled and agreed to meet with me the following week.

When we met, I pitched the idea to him, presented my recommended approach and asked him to hire me. I told him how much I thought the work was worth and a commission structure. He loved it and I started the following week. It was an incredible company to work with. He was an extraordinary visionary and a man on a mission to change the world.

To really get the benefits of putting yourself out there you must embrace these key elements:

- Connection to a higher purpose.
- Connection with yourself.
- And connection with others.

Are you doing that? If you aren't yet, now is the time!

## ❓ Key questions from here:

1. What is your higher purpose? Why are you here on this planet and what have you been put here to do?

2. What are your values? What are the things that drive you? What are the things that are most important to you? When you look around your office or your living room, what are the things that you've spent money on?

3. If you look at your calendar, what are the things that you are spending time on? What are your favorite hobbies?

4. What do you like to do outside of work? Do you like to travel? Do you like to eat? Are you interested in fashion? What music do you like? Do you like to cook? What are all the facets and parts to your identity that show who you are?

5. How confident do you feel in connecting with others?

6. Do you connect with people via text? Do you tend to phone people? Or would you rather email them or message them through social media channels?

7. Do you tend to do voice memos? Do you tend to do video? What forms of communication do you use to connect with other people?

8. On a scale of one to 10, how much energy do you feel like you have towards putting yourself out there?

9. On a scale of one to 10, how excited are the people who are enabling and supporting you to help make these things happen? How excited are they for you?

10. On a scale of one to 10, how engaged are the right people to help you achieve your results? How engaged are they in helping you?

11. Once you answer these questions and understand your own higher purpose and communications, you'll be able to identify where you are on this journey, and be able to determine exactly what you need to do to put yourself in the mindset of putting yourself out there.

# CHAPTER 3

# The Four Derailers That Hold Us Back From Putting Ourselves Out There

> "The most common way people give up their power is thinking that they don't have any."
>
> – **Alice Walker**

In 2008, I started my life again. My husband at the time was having an affair and rather than being guilt-ridden, he was proud of his actions and would tell anyone who would listen about what he was doing. So, I left town, ashamed and embarrassed.

This was also around the time of the GFC and, to add to my upheaval, I couldn't get a job no matter how many I applied for. In fact, applying for jobs was starting to become a full-time job. Nothing seemed to be going right. I moved home to my parent's house and I remember sitting at my parents' dining table and my mother saying to me, "I don't know what you're doing but I think it's time you talked to Centrelink".

Now, I wasn't too embarrassed to do that, but I was already feeling really disempowered. I was feeling like life was out of control. Things were happening where I didn't feel like I had any choices. And I was finding my circumstances hard to change.

So, I decided to take action. I shifted into my "put myself out there" approach and began to concentrate on figuring out what kind of company or role resonated as my dream job. I knew there was someone out there who needed my help. I just needed to find them.

I set out on my goal and approached a company that met those criteria. They had a need for the help I could provide, and they were the kind of company I'd always dreamed of working for. They hired me and it was an excellent fit for both of us.

Putting ourselves out there doesn't always come naturally to all of us. And sometimes we may engage in some self-sabotaging activities that hold us back from stepping into our personal power. In fact, sometimes we don't do it until our back is against the wall and we're forced to. The good news is you don't have to wait until things go wrong.

Below are the four "derailers" or behaviours that often hold people back from stepping into their personal power.

# The Four Derailers to Putting Yourself Out There

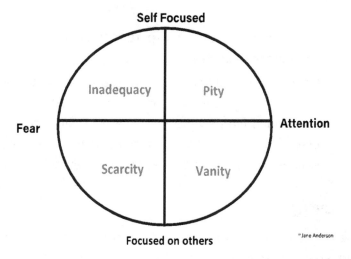

**Self Focused**

Inadequacy | Pity

**Fear** | **Attention**

Scarcity | Vanity

**Focused on others**

" Jane Anderson

## 1. Inadequacy

Have you ever had the feeling you're not good enough? Not smart enough? Maybe you don't have the degree or the experience. Or maybe you don't have a huge social media following, or an extensive email list. Whatever the cause, this sense of inadequacy is sometimes called the "imposter syndrome".

The imposter syndrome is the name for the fear that someone is going to find you out. That someone is going to look around and realise that you don't belong, and you don't deserve to be there.

If this is you (and it's nearly all of us at some point in our careers), your next step is to answer these key questions:

- Have you started to make steps towards your goals?
- Are the fears you have ones that you have created in your own mind?
- Have you spoken to an expert, mentor or coach with experience to advise you?
- Have you actually had a conversation with a decision maker you're wanting to influence? Whether it's for a promotion, a new job or to connect with that ideal client, have you had the conversation with them about what you're trying to do and how you can help them?

## 2. Scarcity

One of the greatest challenges when trying to step out into your space is scarcity. When you are looking at the world from a place of scarcity, you'll find yourself distracted by what everyone else is doing. Worse, you might find yourself worrying that all the opportunities have gone, all the jobs are taken, no-one has the money or can afford to hire you.

If this is you, it's time to see if your assumptions are actually true. Are the jobs really all taken? Have the opportunities all gone? More often than not, it simply isn't true. The jobs are there, and the opportunities as well. But perhaps you need some guidance to know the right way to implement your approach. Maybe you need to put your blinkers on and stop comparing yourself to others. Or maybe you just need to pick up the phone and ask the right people the right questions to see if your assumptions are true?

## 3. Pity

When things don't go the way you want or expect it can be very frustrating. It can seem like no matter what you do, nothing works. You're questioning why this is happening to you or what you've done wrong. And the payoff is that when you share the issue with others, they feel sorry for you, which therefore gains you attention. Maybe you start to enjoy the pity, which leads you to seek it out more and more.

If this is you, it's time to put a deadline on the emotion. It's not going to get you anywhere. Take control by asking for real help if you feel like you can't step out of the situation on your own. Stop being at the peril of your circumstances or playing the victim.

## 4. Vanity

Seeking validation is only natural when gaining a sense of identity. However, when you get that validation for putting out only what's "popular", you aren't necessarily being your most powerful you.

Do you constantly seek likes and comments on your social media feed? Do you need to be reassured all the time? This is not stepping into your power. This is playing the popularity contest and will keep you as a follower not a leader.

## Takeaway

Inadequacy, Scarcity, Pity and Vanity - these are heavy derailers to your ability to effectively put yourself out there. Instead, you should take active steps to avoid these derailers and step into your own power. Once you do, you'll be well and truly on the way to taking control of your business, career and life.

**❓ Key questions from here:**

1. What holds you back from putting yourself out there?
2. What are you most afraid of, really?
3. Which quadrant most resonates for you when putting yourself out there?
4. When was a time when you put yourself out there in the past and it went well?
5. What went well?
6. What would you do if you had your time again?
7. When was a time in the past where it didn't go well?
8. What didn't go well?
9. If you had your time again what would you do differently?
10. If you were to advise someone who may be experiencing the same challenges and fears as you, in putting themselves out there, what advice would you give them?

# CHAPTER 4

# Mind-Hack #1 –
# Get Your Glasses On

"If you are working on something exciting
that you really care about, you don't have
to be pushed. The vision pulls you".

**– Steve Jobs**

## A perfect storm

In the last chapter I talked about starting my life over in 2008.
The ending of my marriage, the start of the GFC, the failure of
traditional job hunting and having to move back home to my
parent's house - all of that led to a perfect storm for me. But
then I got very clear about what my ideal role would be, and I
went after and got that job for my dream company.

That's a great feel-good ending to a hard time in my life. But
how did I do that? How did I get a clear vision for the future?

# Naming my dream

The first thing I had to do was name my dream. If I couldn't get any work, I decided I might as well dream big, because nothing else was working. So, I put together my dream list of qualifications for my dream job. I decided I wanted to run the training department in a large retail company. I wanted them to have a real commitment to training and learning and development, and they needed to be in Brisbane.

# Extending myself

When I knew that I needed to do something different to find my ideal job, the first step I took was to start asking around. Instead of throwing my resume around everywhere, I started asking people who they knew or who met the criteria of the kind of job I was after. The consensus was that I needed to speak to the CEO of a certain company being run in Brisbane at the time. They were going through massive growth, had over 10,000 staff and were also going through major acquisitions at the time. They also had one head recruiter managing their talent pool.

So, I approached the head recruiter and asked her if I could have 10 minutes of her time. I told her that I wanted the opportunity to explain why I thought I might be a good fit for them, even if they weren't recruiting. She said, "Of course. Nobody ever does that. Come and see me". So I went to see her.

The day that we sat down to talk I thanked her for her time, explained what I understood about the organisation and why I thought I would be a good fit. I told her how I thought I could help, the experience that I had, the values fit and, based on what I'd noticed that they were doing, what I thought I could contribute. In the end, she gave me a bit more than 10 minutes, and although they didn't have any jobs at the moment because of the GFC, she asked if we could stay in touch. She said, "I love everything you said and you're spot on. If something comes up, I'll let you know. I really appreciate you coming and talking to me".

It wasn't a traditional success, but to me, it felt like a huge success. I thought, "Thank God I got to talk to a human being". And it was the motivation I needed to keep trying.

So, I went home and started to have more conversations. And two weeks later, I got a call from the recruiter. She said, "We've just had a resignation and we need someone really quickly. I thought of you right away. Are you still interested?" I said, "Absolutely. When can I start?" She said, "Well, you can start tomorrow if you want." I did and I had just landed my dream job.

## Why Does It Matter?

Getting a clear vision for your future helps you to understand the methodology for putting yourself out there. It helps you to see the opportunities and possibilities around you. The opportunities are out there, and if you get clear about what you're after, you'll be more likely to attract them. You'll be more specific, and you'll have more conversations with people who can help you along your path.

In other words, if you don't know what you want, there's no point in putting in any effort to get there. You'd simply be on a road to nowhere.

## Don't wait!

The GFC was a bad time for job hunting – in fact, 250,000 Australians[1] lost their jobs during the crisis. While it was not nearly as bad as 2020 (over 700,000 Australians are estimated to have lost their jobs since March 2020 due to COVID-19[2]), as someone who had always been employed, my confidence was shot. Going through a divorce and starting over added to those vulnerable feelings. I was certainly in a bad place in my life.

And that's an important lesson. We so often wait until things are really bad before we work out what it is that we want. I wish I'd been clearer on my vision much earlier. Of course, after going through a divorce, and starting over, the vision that I'd had for my life before had become muddied. I'd lost my purpose. And it wasn't until I found my clarity again, that I found my vision.

As the psychologist and thinker, Carl Jung said, *"Your vision will become clear only when you can look into your own heart. Who looks outside, dreams; who looks inside, awakes."*

## What are you willing to do?

A critical ingredient for clear vision is knowing what you are willing to do to achieve your goal, and what you are not. Sometimes you have to get yourself out of your comfort zone to get what you are looking for. In my case, I had to stop using traditional job-hunting techniques and try a face-to-face approach. You may need to do something similar in order to really, truly put yourself out there.

The other side of the coin is also knowing exactly what you won't do to achieve your vision. As humans we need balance, and we need to understand where our personal and professional boundaries lie.

Figuring out what you want is important to really, truly and authentically putting yourself out there to build a strong, profitable personal brand.

## ❓ Key questions from here:

1. If you woke up tomorrow and had the dream month, what would it look like?
2. Who would you be working with?
3. Where would you be working?
4. What team would you be in?
5. How much would you be making?
6. What hours would you be working?
7. Where would you live?
8. What type of clients would you have?
9. What type of work would you be doing?
10. Who would you be inspired by?

# CHAPTER 5

# Mind-Hack #2 – Opportunities are Everywhere

*"Opportunities are like buses. There's always another one coming."*

**– Richard Branson**

Recently I was working with a client, Susan, and she said to me, "I feel like I'm giving too much away. I feel like I'm giving a copy of my book, and then I'm giving them my blogs. I'm doing high-touch. I'm doing a lumpy mail. I'm doing all these things". She said, "I'm worried that if I've given them all this stuff, why would they bother to work with me?"

In reality, there's a big difference between the experience of reading the information you've put out into the world and working with you directly.

## The Importance of a Generosity Mindset

It's very important to understand that you can (and should) be generous in giving information and value away. In fact, you've got to create a lot of touch points to get someone to work with you and to trust you. If you're holding back on all that, then you're really giving into that scarcity mindset. Instead of feeling generous, you start to worry, "I'm going to get used. People won't value what I have to say". But actually, the opposite is true. What we're trying to do is get them to see the value that we bring and being generous with your offerings does just that.

The trick is to ensure that your value is available, but also exponentially expanded during the experience of working with you. So, you have to make sure that the value is held there. But what happens is that people hold back. And that step of giving value generously brings people into working with you. It's this content that shows people, "I understand you. I can help you. Here's what I can do".

## What Information Can You Share?

When it comes to sharing your information and assets generously, you are only limited by what you can share that gives your audience value. It could be sharing your knowledge generously over LinkedIn. It could be writing content-rich blog posts. It could be giving them access to your online course for a week or even a month. Once you get them in, once they see what you have to offer, then you can go back to them and ask, "Is this something that would be helpful or not?" This is a particularly good strategy if you're working with B2B and corporate clients.

Alternatively, if you're working with the public market, maybe you can send them a copy of your book. Maybe you could give them some extra tools and resources that they might find useful. Whatever you can do that gives people that sense of, "Wow, she really knows her stuff, and she's so helpful. If this is how generous this person is when I haven't even started to work with them, what must it be like to work with them?"

## Generosity For the Win

My good friend and motivational speaker, Keith Abraham, had a year's worth of speaking events cancelled in his calendar when COVID-19 hit. Rather than sit and complain that over $1 million of work had gone, he simply got on the phone and started to connect with his clients to see what he could do to help.

He went on to deliver 74 presentations for free, not expecting anything in return. Within the following six months his calendar had filled to the same capacity it had in the previous year. His generosity gave his business momentum when the world came back online.

## Generosity, Abundance and Luck

When we talk about generosity, we're talking about more than just giving something to others. Generosity also includes being generous with yourself. It means seeing the best in yourself and expecting good things (and great opportunities) to come your way. It means embracing a mindset of abundance as well as one of luck. This is especially important when it comes to putting yourself out there.

Jill Konrath is the author of *Selling to Big Companies*, and a great proponent of the abundance mindset. She has a strategy for getting in with big companies and that is to simply "act like you're already working with them". Having a sense of positive delusion can help in pretending in your own mind that it's already happening. In other words, imagining that you're already living in abundance, is a great first step to actually getting there.

This has worked for me. At one point when I was really struggling in my practice, I spent six months pretending I was doing $1 million dollar days. I'd be working from home but I'd wear the most expensive suits, shoes and jewellery. I got out all my good china and started to use it every day. I just pretended that I was working in a space of abundance. It was a mind hack that worked well for me, by helping me to play in abundance and removing the sense of lack that was overwhelming me.

But abundance is just one part of it. In fact, a big part of having an abundant mindset is feeling lucky. Dr Richard Wisemann wrote a book called *The Luck Factor* and in it he talks about the studies that he completed around the luck mindset. In one study he placed actors in a coffee shop, one of whom appeared to be a successful businessman, and a five pound note just outside. Each person walked in, and one immediately saw the five pound note, picked it up, went in, ordered his coffee and then struck up a conversation with the businessman. The next person who came in did not see the note and simply sat quietly next to the businessman without engaging in any conversation.

When the two people were interviewed later the first believed himself to be incredibly lucky (he had won a huge lottery pot previously) while the second considered herself clumsy, unattractive and extremely unlucky. But it was those mindsets that seemed to attract the luck (or non-luck) as well as opportunities that the luck brought (conversations with a successful businessman, for example).

This was only one of Wisemann's studies, but this outcome is proved over and over again. Those people who had a "lucky" mindset actually have more luck.[3]

Wisemann's research showed that lucky people generate their own good fortune because they're skilled at creating and noticing opportunities, they make lucky decisions because they listen (and believe in) their own intuition, they have a resilient attitude and they create self-fulfilling prophecies because of their positive expectations. And these things transform bad luck into good luck.

Finding your own luck doesn't mean just sitting around and waiting. It involves taking action. When I started my own practice I started to think about the dream clients I'd like to work with. So, I reached out to them and offered to work for free. I wrote LinkedIn profiles for some of the most experienced experts in their field. I sent them personal videos showing them opportunities in their profiles and to see if I could help and at no charge. As a result of the success they achieved from their profiles, I was invited to masterminds and to do presentations and was introduced to more clients than I could handle. This strategy set my practice up for success and was worth every moment of writing those profiles.

As Wisemann said, "The concept of luck is very straightforward. Some people notice opportunities, and others don't".

## Research Backed

Having a generosity mindset, including abundance and luck, isn't just a nice to have. It's proven to lead to higher profitability. In fact, research undertaken by Dr Nathan Podsakoff at the University of Arizona on nearly 40 studies of organisational behaviour, found that there is a surprisingly strong link between employee generosity and desirable business outcomes.[4] The research showed the more generous employees were, the more their area showed higher profitability, productivity, efficiency, customer satisfaction, lower costs and lower turnover rates.[5] It's also linked to more efficient problem solving, team coordination and a cohesive, supportive working culture.[6] All good things.

## Managing Your Generosity

While a generosity mindset is a necessary part of building your personal brand, you do have to manage it. One of the biggest challenges you can face is being too accommodating. When you're too generous and too accommodating, you might find that you are interrupting your own workflow for paying clients, fielding constant interruptions in order to help people out. If you don't stand up for yourself and manage your own time and resources, you can easily find yourself pushed into the "friend-toring" space, which is not productive or helpful.

The key is to manage the boundaries of your generosity, so that you are able to help people out, but maintain your own productivity and efficiency.

## There's Enough for Everyone

It's easy to be pulled into thoughts that you're being ripped off. Or that there isn't enough work, opportunities or clients to go around. But the truth is that there are enough. Your generosity (within manageable limits), abundance and luck mindsets will ensure that you are reaching those clients and finding those opportunities.

### 🛈 Key questions from here:

1. On a scale of one to 10, answer the question, "How generous am I in my mindset in giving people tools, resources and things to help them?" 10 being, "I'm ridiculously generous. I've nailed it.' And one being, "I'm just not generous enough. I'm afraid of being taken advantage of".

2. Who do you admire as being a generous person?

3. What do they do to demonstrate generosity and abundance?

4. How does that make you feel?

5. In what areas do you feel a sense of scarcity?

6. What are you afraid of losing?

7. How could you feel more abundant?

8. Who is your ideal client?

9. If you could reach out to them today, what could you do to help them for free? What do they need right now?

10. What would it mean for you to have your dream client on board?

# CHAPTER 6

# Mind-Hack #3 – Crush Comparisonitis

*"Comparison is a brutal assault upon one's self. Once you compare yourself to someone else, what you're really saying is that what you're made of isn't good enough."*

**– Cameron Diaz**

Comparisonitis (noun): The compulsion to compare one's accomplishments to another's to determine relative importance.

I remember the day like it was yesterday. It was about four years ago at an event. I delivered my keynote, was mingling and answering questions, and smiling all the way through. But the entire time I felt this weight crushing me. It was almost suffocating.

And it just would not. Let. Up.

The feeling was familiar. It was a persistent feeling of being found out. I had this heavy feeling that people were suddenly going to realise that I wasn't good enough, smart enough or clever enough. I was around all these incredible influencers and industry leaders and thinking 'what on earth could I have to offer'.

My thoughts went like this:

> "All the books have been written on the subjects I want to write about."

> "There are other experts who help people on the things I do."

> "There aren't enough clients out there to work with me.

> "And anyway... why would they work with me when they could work with her (or him)?"

I knew my thinking was wrong but I just couldn't seem to shake it. So, I smiled and chatted to people, trying to manage the conversations and hope that my fear wasn't noticeable. I felt like I was in the wrong room at first and just didn't belong, yet knew I needed to stay and it took all my strength to not walk out the door. It was like having a new pair of school shoes on the first day of school - awkward and uncomfortable.

## Imposter Syndrome

We've talked about the imposter syndrome in this book already. But it bears repeating because this lack of self-belief is debilitating and exhausting. It's stressful and frustrating and it can be utterly relentless with a grip so tight you can't fight it. And that's exactly what I was experiencing in that room.

What I didn't know then that I know now is that in all likelihood a great proportion of people in that room were feeling those same feelings. In fact, a study undertaken by Pauline Clance, found that women frequently say that they don't feel they deserve their job and that they are "imposters" who could be found out at any moment.[7] They found that women worry more about being disliked, appearing unattractive, outshining others or grabbing too much attention.[8]

Men are not exempt from doubting themselves either, of course—they just don't let their doubts stop them as often as women do. A Hewlett Packard internal report (reported by *Harvard Business Review*) found that men apply for a job or promotion when they meet only 60% of the qualifications, but women apply only if they meet 100% of them.[9] What doomed them was not their actual ability, but rather the decision not to try.[10] The decision to not try can often stem from us assuming that we aren't going to be as good or compare as well as others in the applicant pool.

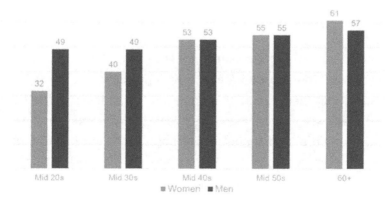

# Comparisonitis

Zenger Folkman's research above shows that as women's experience increases over time, so does their confidence.[11] The graph shows that women's confidence increases more with age than men's.[12] It makes me wonder how many opportunities are lost in the early years of women's careers because of comparisonitis, fear and lack of confidence.

Imposter syndrome is a part of comparisonitis, both arising from, and causing it. When we let ourselves believe that everyone else is better than we are, then we begin to doubt our abilities, our strengths, our skills and our knowledge. We get lost in the feeling that we can't compete.

## Let go of perfectionism

Are you a recovering perfectionist? I know I certainly am. And when you're putting yourself out there, it's a pretty vulnerable space to be. It's easy to look around and judge yourself against others in your space. But to crush comparisonitis and play your own game you have to let go of perfectionism.

## Why we sink into perfectionism

Letting go of perfectionism is not that easy. We want to *look* perfect so that we can *feel* like we can compete. We try to project this perception to people and that feels important because we are selling ourselves and selling ourselves is very different to trying to sell any other kind of product. Selling ourselves comes with more risk of vulnerability and with an added fear of rejection. That causes us to sink into perfectionism as we try to make everything perfect so people like us and want to work with us.

## Comparisonitis Goes Both Ways

Comparisonitis isn't just a problem for you. When you paint yourself as perfect, other people around you will go into comparison mode,too. They go into the mindset where they begin to think, "I'm not sure that I'm good enough to work with her. I'm not sure that she would like me. I'm not sure that I'm good enough to be around that person". And that problem then becomes your problem as well. People don't want to work with people that seem too perfect.

On the other hand, if you can tap into your authenticity and let go of the need to be perfect just a little bit, you will actually appeal to people more. When you paint yourself as perfect, people go into comparison, but if you're authentic, people go into possibility. Suddenly they stop worrying about how they will stack up next to you and start thinking, "Wow, she's just like me. She's so much more real, authentic or genuine than I thought she was going to be, or he was going to be. And I do things like that, too".

This authenticity creates a greater sense of real connection, and when you can tap into that, you can create a deeper sense of belief for your own clients. Those clients then start to really think, "OK, well maybe I can do this. Maybe I can get the results that I'm looking for. This feels a little bit more achievable and it feels like I could actually do something here".

## Managing Comparisonitis

As Mark Twain said, *"Comparison is the thief of joy"*. But it is also the thief of strong, successful personal branding and it will thwart your ability to really put yourself out there. In order to engage well with your audience, you need to beat comparisonitis on both levels - within yourself, and within your audience. And that means you need strategies to manage it.

Here are four strategies that you might find helpful if you're feeling like you're suffering under the weight of comparisonitis:

1. **Ask for help.** Speak to a support person, friend, family or professional who can help you to put strategies in place if you don't know what to do. There's absolutely no shame in asking. I had a mentor who was earning 10 times in a day what I was at one point, and she said, "Remember, I have been doing this for 10 years. I was where you are now at one point. You'll get here someday, too. I believe in you". And I did. In fact, I ended up earning more than 50% more than her.

2. **Be your own best friend.** Research shows that 80% of our self talk is negative. Catch your negative self-talk and reframe it to speak to yourself nicely. Instead of saying "you idiot" when you make a mistake, just say, "Oops, that was funny", or "Geez, I crack myself up".

3. **Remember your uniqueness.** There is only one of you. Sure, others might deliver similar work to you but they can't replicate your essence.

4. **Create before you consume.** I got this one from the author, Marie Forleo. Celebrate and amplify your

uniqueness by creating. Whether it's videos, a book, a blog… whatever. Just get creating as people will come to you because you can connect with them at a deeper level. Become as fully self-expressed as possible by showing us what you care about.

5. **Disconnect to reconnect.** Get off social media for a while, a week even. Get back to you and stop looking at what everyone else is doing.

# ❓ Key questions from here:

1. Who are you comparing yourself to?

2. What are you comparing? Brand, content, photography, story, family, clients, location, revenue?

3. How do you know that what you are comparing yourself to is actually true?

4. Who do you need to unsubscribe from, unfollow and disconnect from?

5. What are you saying to yourself when you catch yourself putting yourself down? How have you reframed your language to yourself?

6. How would your friends or colleagues describe your essence? Your energy?

7. Turn off notifications on your phone and just have text messages coming in and use notifications from your calendar. What do you notice?

8. Spend the first two hours of your day tomorrow creating something that brings you joy. What do you notice?

9. How often do you speak down to yourself (i.e., ugh you're an idiot, you're so stupid, so fat etc..)?

10. What kind words could you say to yourself instead?

# CHAPTER 7

# Mind-Hack #4 –
# Fly With Eagles

"Surround yourself only with
people who will lift you higher."

**– Oprah**

I don't know about you, but I don't really watch much TV. But one thing I do love to watch is *The Voice*. The mix of talent, both from the performers and coaches, astounds me and I always wonder if they have decided which coach they want to work with before they go on stage (I assume they have!).

When I watch Kylie, Will.I.Am, Ricky and Joel, I find it fascinating how they pitch their USP (unique selling proposition) and explain why the individuals should choose to work with them. Each sells their expertise and what makes them most relevant to the contestant achieving their dreams so they will pick them. I often use *The Voice* as the example when I ask people if they have a mentor.

First of all, when it comes to building a strong personal brand, and learning to put yourself out there, I believe you need to have a mentor. I have been fortunate to have wonderful mentors in my life, both paid and unpaid. Mentors save us time by helping us find the pathway we need quickly. They save us mistakes and open us up to their networks. Without them it may take a long time to get any traction and it's a big effort to make things happen.

Mentors are a great way to create advocates and sponsors for you. They will often look for ways to help by introducing you to people, sharing opportunities and growing your network through them.

## How to Find the Right Mentor

The rules of finding the right mentor are:

1. **Know your goal.** Be clear about what you're trying to achieve for the next 12 months. 90 days is too short for a strong mentor relationship and five years is too long. Just focus on what you want by the end of the year. For example, if your goal is to improve your networks then find a mentor who not only does that well but can articulate and show you how they do it.

2. **Look for the person who has done "that" already.** Ask your friends, colleagues, Facebook mates or LinkedIn connections, or even Google it or Tweet it. Industry bodies can also be a good place to start. You're not just looking for any mentor. You're looking for the one that will help you achieve that goal (whatever "that" is) that you're hoping to nail.

3. **Ask if they mentor people.** Once you've found the right person you may have to pay them for their time. This is an investment in your future and the reason that person has been able to do it means they are successful and likely very busy. A coffee or buying lunch for them is not always going to cut it. Alternatively, you can offer to do something for them like helping them on a project. It has taken them years to work out what you're wanting to learn in an hour, so be respectful of the value they bring.

4. **Rapport is key.** Make sure you like and trust them. They don't have to be your best friend but it's going to be an open conversation at times. Make sure you're comfortable to work with them.

## Why It Matters

Finding a great mentor can really help you leverage your experience to build your personal brand. More importantly, they can show you what works well (and what doesn't) within your industry. You don't have to make all the same mistakes that they have. And you can feel more confident, and be more successful, putting yourself out there when you have their years of experience and expert advice behind you, supporting you to achieve your goals.

## 🗨️ Key questions from here:

1. What goal would you like to achieve in the next 12 months?
2. How committed are you to achieving that goal?
3. Who do you know who has already achieved that goal? Think of people you know personally and don't know personally.
4. Do they take on mentees (paid and unpaid)?
5. If you need to pay, identify what the value would be to you.
6. If you had the opportunity to meet with them, what would be the number one thing you want to learn from them?
7. How would you know you've been successful in achieving that goal?
8. How long do they think it might take to learn?
9. Whilst mentors might seem like they have it all, what can you help your mentor to achieve? (Hint: you might need to ask them.)
10. How often will you be meeting with them?

# CHAPTER 8

# Mind-Hack #5 – Celebrate Your Nos

"Every no gets me closer to a yes."
**– Mark Cuban**

I remember it like it was yesterday.

I was sitting at my desk in my home office in late 2016 and my good friend Simon called. He and I were in a sales training course and both working on improving our ability to overcome the fear of sales calls. He was procrastinating and calling me to say hi and see how I was going.

I explained to him that I had been filling out my tracker and monitoring the numbers and that I was just finding it hard to keep the motivation up. He asked me to go through my numbers and kindly listened to my complaining. And then he stopped me and said:

"You know what? Can I make an observation?

"Sure", I said.

"What I'm hearing is that you're focused on the outcome and not on the task. You know that what you're doing is right, you just have really high expectations for yourself and you're so focused on people saying 'yes'. This seems to be creating a lot of pressure for you and that might be sending pressure and desperation to your customer, impacting your sales calls. Have you thought about focussing on the 'nos'?"

I stopped and had to think about what he was asking me. Then I said, "Of course I'm not focussed on the nos. I want yesses!"

He said, "Well, if the targets you've set are right, all you need to do is get through potentially nine 'nos' to get to one 'yes'. So, just celebrate the progress of getting through your nos and you'll get a yes at some stage anyway".

This was life changing advice for me. I'd never thought about it this way.

## Celebrating Your Nos

As American billionaire and entrepreneur Mark Cuban says, *"The word 'no' leads many of us to see it as a failure. 'No' comes in different forms: the test you just failed, the interview that didn't lead to a job and the person who tells you 'you can't'. We look at that 'no' often enough to never go near it again.*

*'No' does not mean defeat, however. It is an opportunity to get closer to the 'yes' for which you are searching. Do not let the 'nos' of life impact your goals.*

'Nos' are part of your story, and if you keep working hard, they will lead to many 'yeses', which often turn out to be better than the opportunities for which the 'nos' would have provided."

## Activity Cures Inactivity

So, being able to create a mind-hack to focus more on nos and less on yesses means we can focus on activity. And as my good friend and godfather of speaking in Australia, Keith Abraham says, "Activity cures inactivity".

In the course I was in we ran a study at one point to identify the value of a meeting. The data was taken from over 150 people and the measure was taken on the number of sales and the number of sales meetings. We determined that even a meeting where nothing was sold was worth $2,450. So, even if the client said 'no', there was still a lot of value in the meeting. This again blew my mind and made me realise the value of each person I spoke to and how even the nos would get me closer to a yes.

This meant so many things!

1. A surrendering to the process and letting go.
2. Less pressure and trusting the process.
3. Showing up more authentically.
4. Being lighter and less attached to the outcome.

## A Growth Mindset

At this time I also purchased the book *Mindset* by Carol Dweck. Her research on what she calls a *"growth mindset"* identifies that people improve their performance over time by focusing less on the result and more on their effort and progress.[13]

This can be useful along with questions like, "How many more no's did you get today than yesterday?" And I can certainly vouch that this was a powerful shift, not just in mindset but for my own mental health.

Carol says, *"In a growth mindset challenges are exciting rather than threatening. So rather than thinking, 'oh, I'm going to reveal my weaknesses', you say 'here's a chance to grow'".*[14]

And I think she's spot on. We really do need to keep looking at how far we've come and less about how far we still have to go to being perfect.

## Keep Putting Yourself Out There, Despite the Nos

Know that you're going to get no's, no matter what you do and continue putting yourself out there. If you don't ask, you don't get, right? And if you don't put yourself out there, you won't build your brand, your business or your revenue. So, look forward to the no's knowing they're bringing you closer to a yes!

## ❓ Key questions from here:

1. What's the goal you're trying to achieve? (More sales? A job?)

2. How many people do you need to reach out to?

3. How many no's do you expect to get?

4. What is the value of a no to you?

5. Decide on how you'll celebrate your nos (e.g., a massage after you've achieved 50)?

6. What else do you need to do to elevate your mindset when hitting nos?

7. What are you getting a chance to grow in your business, career or life right now?

8. How far have you come since you tried this a day, week, month or year ago?

9. Where have you been putting more effort in over the last month or year?

10. How are you going to celebrate this?

# CHAPTER 9

# Mind-Hack #6 –
# Embrace Your Uniqueness

> "In order to be irreplaceable, one
> must always be different."
>
> **– Coco Chanel**

If you've ever seen an Angostura Bitters bottle with its oversized white label, you'll know it's pretty distinctive. But many people don't know the story behind the bottle's appearance. And it's a story worth telling.

When Dr Johann Siegert died in 1870, his two sons took over the already established bitters business. They wanted to expand the business and gain more widespread attention, so they decided to enter a bitters competition in order to showcase their product's quality to the world.

In preparation for the competition one brother was in charge of designing a new bottle and the other of designing a new label. Unfortunately, they didn't consult each other about sizing and when the new labels and bottles arrived, the label was too big.

It was too late for them to make any changes, so they entered the competition with their bottle covered in the oversized label. They lost the competition, but one of the judges encouraged them to keep their "signature labelling".

They did, and since then all Angostura bottles are made and shipped with this recognisable and iconic piece of packaging.

## Fear Makes Us Vanilla

The things that make us unique and different can sometimes feel like "faults" as well. Often we're afraid of showing our own "oversized labels". We fear being vulnerable, of showing our soft underbelly, of letting the world see who we really are. And we're afraid of oversharing and losing credibility because we aren't perfect.

So, we try to hide the things that make us stand out from the crowd in an effort to be seen as "just like everyone else". Or we try to shoehorn ourselves into some kind of one-size-fits-all brand with air-brushed images and bland messages.

The problem with trying to fit in is, that that's just what we end up doing. Our brand becomes vanilla, our voice watered down and our messaging vague and uninspiring. No one hears us or sees us because we're lost in a sea of people doing, saying and being the same things. In our search for perfectionism, we lose ourselves.

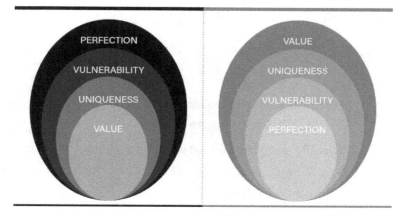

## Perfectionism is Bad for Us – Personally and Professionally

We talked a little bit about perfectionism in the last chapter in terms of comparisonitis, but it bears repeating here. Because perfectionism doesn't just make you vanilla and bland, it's also bad for you.

Perfectionism is linked with depression[15], anxiety[16], self-harm[17], social anxiety disorder[18], agoraphobia[19], obsessive-compulsive disorder[20], binge eating[21], anorexia[22], bulimia[23], post-traumatic stress disorder[24], chronic fatigue syndrome[25], insomnia[26], chronic headaches[27], early mortality[28] and even suicide[29].

Professionally, it holds you back from being your most productive self. It keeps you from sharing your most important and valuable messages. And it stops you from resonating with the right people.

# How to Recognise Perfectionism

Perfectionism doesn't always look how you think. Lynne Cazaly, in her book, *ish*, talks about three types of perfectionism:

1. **Self-oriented perfectionism** is holding yourself to impossibly high standards.

2. **Socially-prescribed perfectionism** is perceiving that others have unreasonable expectations for you.

3. **Other-oriented perfectionism** is where you place excessively high standards on others.

Research shows that over the past almost 20 years, each type of perfectionism has been on the rise with the second type increasing the most – by a whopping 33%.[30] Researchers say that the cultures they studied – American, Canadian and British – are all becoming "more and more individualised, materialistic and socially antagonistic".[31]

Brené Brown says, *"Perfectionism is a self-destructive and addictive belief system that fuels this primary thought: If I look perfect, and do everything perfectly, I can avoid or minimise the painful feelings of shame, judgment, and blame".*

# Why Does It Matter

When you seek out perfectionism, you can only fail. Nobody is perfect. That inevitable failure opens you up to comparisonitis (as discussed earlier) both in yourself and in your audience. I've said it before - people don't want to work with perfect people.

Instead, they want to work with people that they can relate to, that feel authentic and able to understand them and their challenges. An *imperfect* person can do that.

## Overcoming Perfectionism

The Siegert brothers were faced with a problem, an error, even a fault. But rather than succumbing to what could be a disaster, they embraced their "problem" and turned it into an asset. What made them unique, made them interesting and made them memorable.

Your uniqueness is what makes you interesting. It's what helps you stand out from the crowd and find your voice. Importantly, being yourself, embracing yourself is not just good for your brand and your business, but for your own personal health and wellbeing.

## Put Yourself Out There - Warts and All

To be a healthy and successful human, you have to learn from your mistakes, and that means you have to be comfortable making them in the first place. Personal growth is essential for wellbeing, and professional growth is essential for business success. So, we need to put ourselves out there, warts and all, make mistakes and grow and learn from them.

You will make mistakes. You will do things that are quirky and unusual. You may not always follow the crowd, but those aren't bad things, and they can be great things. Your uniqueness makes you special. Embracing it and sharing it can build your brand, engage your audience and engender loyalty. Just like Angostura Bitters' mistake did for them.

 **Key questions from here:**

1. What makes you different from your competition? If you're not sure, ask your clients.
2. How are you amplifying this?
3. What aspects of you are you most uncomfortable with?
4. In what areas is perfectionism holding you back?
5. What activities outside of your work do you feel the most joyful and free to be your most authentic self?
6. Which brands or people do you admire who are at their most authentic and imperfect? Why?
7. How often do you undertake these activities?
8. How can you include them more?
9. How often do you hang out with people who have the vulnerability to be their most authentic selves?
10. If a friend or colleague came to you to ask for advice on how to embrace their uniqueness, what advice would you give them?

# CHAPTER 10

# Mind-Hack #7 – Be Vulnerably You

*"Vulnerability is not about winning or losing. It's about having the courage to show up when you can't control the outcome."*

**– Brené Brown**

Most of us don't trust anything that seems a bit too perfect (and that includes people, as we've touched on before). In the age of social media and the way that we consume information, the more real something is the more we tend to trust it. And the challenge for a lot of leaders and entrepreneurs is that when we attach our self-worth to whatever we are delivering, trying to be real becomes even more challenging.

I was recently delivering a presentation to a government department and one of the very senior executive leaders introduced me. During that introduction they shared their personal journey of experiencing mental health challenges and suffering depression, acknowledging that it was common knowledge in their workplace.

In fact, when I asked a number of people who were there, they said that her experiences were well known. But rather than finding that off-putting, everyone I spoke to said that they found her more real, and very connected to the challenges that they experienced in their own jobs. Even more, they were inspired that she was able to continue on, not only as a leader, but as a female leader. They felt respected, and they didn't feel as embarrassed or as ashamed to speak up when they were going through a tough time themselves. A number of them said they felt more empowered to know their value and worth in their own wellbeing and ability to do their job.

Still, being vulnerable can feel hard.

## Why Vulnerability Matters

Being able to show a side of you that may not be strong in a world where we're trying to be powerful, resilient and lead change seems counterintuitive. But when we have a greater sense of vulnerability ourselves, and share that vulnerability, we allow others to become vulnerable, connected, lighter, open and transparent, and, therefore, create greater trust.

Vulnerability creates a deeper connection than just a surface level conversation. While being vulnerable we harness the power to be able to share openly and we're not as afraid of doing things wrong. In fact, it breeds innovation and trying and testing things, as opposed to being afraid of change or of something not going right and trying to keep the status quo.

I deliver a Business and Leadership program called **Women with Influence** where we have a laugh about our failures that week. We call it "F'UP Friday". We not only laugh at ourselves but also share our learnings as part of the failure. In fact, my own team uses it and it has created permission to have the conversation that we're not perfect. We find out about mistakes in a safe way and are able to fix them without the person feeling like they're incompetent or will get in trouble.

## Removing the Wall Between You and Your Clients

When you are vulnerable it's like removing an invisible wall that's between you and your team or you and your clients. The wall is them thinking that they're not good enough or smart enough. But if you can remove that wall it means that you're far more connected as a team and there is much greater trust. As a result you gain more traction, more motivation and, therefore, transformation.

## Daring Greatly

Brené Brown is the master of doing work around her own vulnerability. She wrote the book, *Daring Greatly - How the Courage to be Vulnerable Transforms the Line We Live, Love, Parent, and Lead.*

In her **Ted Talk,** 'The Power of Vulnerability', which is one of the most viewed Ted Talks of all time with over 30 million views,[32] Brené talks about how she's been able to embrace her own vulnerability. She shares stories of people she's worked with and based on her 12 years of research covers courage, worthiness and shame.

She says, *"We can't know things like love and belonging and joy and creativity without vulnerability"*.

## The Armour of Perfectionism

Brown says that the thing that holds us back from being vulnerable is the armour of perfectionism. Perfectionism is, at its core, about trying to earn approval. She says that most perfectionists grew up being praised for achievement and performance through their grades at school, their manners, following rules, pleasing people, how they dress and they're sporting abilities. She says they are raised to understand that they will get praised if they get a great result. And that leads to a desire to be perfect.[33]

As we've mentioned before, perfectionism is directly correlated with depression, anxiety, addiction, paralysis and missing opportunities. The fear of failing, of making mistakes, of not meeting people's expectations and of being criticised leads us to an area where there is unhealthy competition. Perfectionism is not a way to avoid being vulnerable or avoiding feeling ashamed.

Brown says perfectionism is a form of shame. When we struggle with perfectionism we're actually really struggling with shame. She says that vulnerability is not knowing victory or defeat, it's understanding the necessity of both. It's engaging. It's being all in.[34]

# Being All In

People who put themselves out there in support of their business and personal brand are embracing change, and this can lead to them experiencing fear. They may feel anxious, stressed and like things are maybe out of their control. To combat this they have to be *all in*. We have to be *all in*. But the only way to be *all in* is to be vulnerable to be able to share our fullest selves.

When we are vulnerable then we can then have an even deeper authentic connection with our clients and audience. We have stronger credibility and greater empathy for the experiences that our clients are going through. And everyone feels a sense of safety.

## You Are Powerful Beyond Measure

Of course, it was **Marianne Williamson** who said:

> *"Our deepest fear is not that we are inadequate. Our deepest fear is that we are powerful beyond measure. It is our light, not our darkness, that frightens us and we ask ourselves, who am I to be brilliant, gorgeous, and fabulous. Well who are you not to be? You are a child of God. Your playing small does not serve the world. There is nothing enlightened about shrinking so that others don't feel so insecure around you. You were meant to shine, as children do, and you were born to manifest the glory of God that is within us but it's not within some of us but is within everyone and when we let our light shine we give others permission*

*to do the same. And when we have liberated our fear,*
*our presence automatically liberates others."*

## Putting Yourself Out There With Vulnerability

It's probably pretty clear why being vulnerable is a necessary part of "putting yourself out there". In fact, when you are putting yourself out there, you will likely be feeling vulnerable. But there is a difference between simply feeling that uncomfortable feeling, and embracing it until you do feel comfortable.

The first doesn't feel very good. But the second gives you the ability to connect with your clients, to expand on their sense of safety with you and to create a space where people feel engaged with you, understanding from you and a feeling that you'll understand them when things go awry. That's what the senior executive did when she opened up about her struggles with mental health. What can you share today?

## ❓ Key questions from here:

1. Who do you need help from right now?

2. Who do you admire who has shared their failures in the past?

3. What have been some of the failures that you have had in the past?

4. How do you feel about them now?

5. Which ones do you need more time to process?

6. Which ones could you share with your audience?

7. Who is a safe and experienced person for you to share a vulnerable experience with?

8. When could you share it with them?

9. What feedback have they given you?

10. What advice would you give someone who is afraid of sharing their failures and fears?

# CHAPTER 11

# Mind-Hack #8 – It's Not All About You!

*"Humility is not thinking less of yourself;
it's about thinking about yourself less."*

**– CS Lewis**

Many years ago, in the 90s, I had a music teacher whose name was Tom. He was a beautiful pianist and was often asked to play at important events and in amazing venues. In fact, around that time a mutual friend asked him to come and play at her wedding which was to be held at the Stamford Plaza (the most elite and luxurious hotel in Brisbane at the time).

Tom had gone to the hotel a bit early and made his way down to the gym to put in a little time on the treadmill. After a while a lovely African-American woman got on the treadmill next to him. They soon struck up a conversation. During the course of the conversation she asked him what he was there for, and he told her he was playing the piano for a friend's wedding. Soon they were both done working out, and they headed on their way.

Later that night, Tom was standing near the front of the hotel after the wedding when a caravan of cars with police escorts and paparazzi pulled up in front of the hotel. The woman from the hotel gym got out of the car, and Tom finally recognised her – it was Macy Gray – one of the most famous musicians at the time.

She started to make her way into the hotel followed by her large entourage, including photographers and screaming fans when Ms Gray spotted Tom standing nearby. She immediately called out amongst the chaos saying (to his great astonishment), "Hey, Tom! How was your gig?!"

Why is this such a wonderful story? Because Macy Gray had just played at a stadium with over 50,000 fans. Yet, she was humble and aware enough to make her contact with Tom about him.

## How to Stay Humble in Your Content

One of the things that many people struggle with when creating content, is how to put themselves in their content and still stay humble. Many want to share their successes and wins with their community (and they should) but worry about bragging or coming across as egotistical.

In fact, that intuition is right. Usually, the people who struggle with this worry, have excellent interpersonal skills. They recognise that putting their accomplishments in their content could look like they were just trying to draw attention to themselves. And they worry it could come across as self-serving.

But it doesn't have to work that way. Here's how to put yourself in your content without bragging.

## Reframe the Issue

The best way to combat the appearance of bragging is to shift the attention from yourself to the problem you want to solve and who needs it solved. In other words, you reframe the issue to **why what you do matters** rather than why you are so great.

Let's imagine you're in a business etiquette role and you've been asked to present at an influential conference. Rather than putting up a post that says, "On my way to present at this conference, so excited!", instead focus on why the conference itself is important.

You could say, "Women face more challenges than men getting their ideas heard at work[35]. It's more important than ever to make our voices heard and be able to make a difference". Then you can turn this back to yourself and say, "I'm incredibly grateful to be able to speak about getting your voice heard at this Women in Finance conference recently, working with 300 female leaders in an industry going through major change post Royal Commission. There is no more important time than now for their voices to be heard to lead change in the industry".

You are still sharing your accomplishment and your success, but you are doing it in a way that highlights the message and the audience rather than yourself.

## Shine the spotlight

Another way to look at it is the spotlight model (or we could even call it "the Macy Gray model"). When you are successful or great things are happening to you, you already have a spotlight shining on you. You've created your brand and your platform and draw that success and spotlight to you. So, now it is your role to shine the light on the message, or even on to someone else.

That is exactly what Macy Gray did. She was already in the spotlight, she didn't need to draw more attention to herself. And by turning the light on Tom, she gave him a chance to shine. And, of course, it didn't dim her own light at all.

# 3 Steps to Writing Humble Content

## How to Put Yourself out There Without Bragging

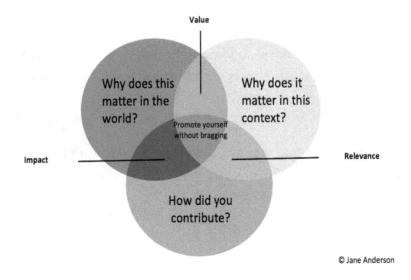

© Jane Anderson

1. **Value.** Why does what you do matter?
2. **Relevance.** Why did it matter in this context?
3. **Impact.** What did you do?

Creating content that doesn't appear self-serving, egotistical or like bragging is the goal. And when your content hits that sweet spot where value, relevance and impact meet, you will be doing just that. Tell your audience **why it matters** (because women haven't had a voice in the workplace), **why it's relevant** (there's a conference dealing with this issue) and only then **what impact you had** (you're presenting there).

## Humble Leaders Are the Leaders of Tomorrow

Humility is essential to leadership and to building your brand. Humility connects us with others at a human level. It creates an atmosphere of trust, respect and equality. And it sets up an environment where everyone and every business can succeed.

> "The difference between a good leader and a great leader is humility."
> – Jim Collins

Now that you've found success, it is essential to lead others with humility, shining the spotlight on their own successes and achievements. This is also a fantastic way to put yourself out there.

## ❓ Key questions from here:

1. Look at the last 10 posts on your social media - how many times do you use the word "I"?

2. Now find ways to replace and remove the word "I" in your copy.

3. Now ask yourself the question: "Why does this post matter?" In other words, what does the research say about this topic? Why should your audience care?

4. What specific problem does your audience have in relation to this topic? What would they say is their problem (not what you think their issue is)?

5. Add this challenge to the beginning to frame your content.

6. Share the previous version and the new version with an ideal audience member.

7. Ask them which one connects more.

8. What did they say?

9. What insight did you learn?

# CHAPTER 12

# Mind-Hack #9 – Get Comfortable With Discomfort

> "The biggest rewards in life are found outside your comfort zone. Live with it. Fear and risk are prerequisites if you want to enjoy a life of success and adventure."
>
> **– Jack Canfield**

I want to talk about the C-word... the 'comfort' zone. I know that's what you were thinking. You *were* thinking that, weren't you?

## What is the Comfort Zone?

Your comfort zone in this case isn't when you're snuggled up on the couch with a glass of wine. What we're talking about here is the psychological state where things feel familiar and easy to you, and where you feel in control of what is happening. For each of us that will be a different place. Delivering a keynote to 1000 people might be in the comfort zone for one person, and not for another. Or writing and publishing articles on LinkedIn might be comfortable for your colleagues, but not for you. The area covered is vast and completely different for each individual.

But one key thing to note about your comfort zone is that when you are operating within this space, you are only capable of a steady level of performance. In other words, you aren't going to be kicking any goals or making any waves from your comfort zone.

This is highlighted by the quote from John Assaraf, world-leading mindset and behaviour expert, where he says, "*The comfort zone is a beautiful place, but nothing grows there*". And he's right.

A few years ago, my youngest sister Carmen called me from a remote area in Western Australia. She said that she wanted to come back over to the Eastern side of the country and, in particular wanted to move back to Canberra. She asked if I could help her apply for jobs in Canberra in the department where she was working, which happened to be the Federal Police. Of course I said I would help her and so she started to send me job ads of roles that were being advertised.

When I read them, I asked her if she was actually interested in these roles. She replied saying no not really, but she just really wanted to move back to Canberra regardless and she was happy to compromise on the type of role.

So, I asked her what she wanted to do, if she could do anything.

She said that she would ideally love to go back to Canberra and into a training role in the department. She was previously a teacher and loved teaching. So, I said "Why don't you ask for that?" To which she replied "But that's not what they're looking for. There are no ads for that type of role".

I asked her if she had spoken with anyone there to find out if there were any training opportunities. She had always thought that with government roles you needed to wait until something was advertised. I had been a HR Advisor in government a few years prior and I said to her that anything was possible. I asked her if she would get on a plane at her own expense, go to Canberra and speak to people proactively and not sit back and wait.

She said she would.

So, we came up with a plan. We designed the ideal role, the metrics of success and how it would contribute to the department.

She then called the head of learning and development for the department and said that she was interested in moving back to Canberra and wanted to see him and asked if he would meet with her. He agreed.

She put together her pitch and by the end of the meeting he said "I don't have any roles at the moment but we have a need for someone to take on a project in the training division for six months. Would you be interested in taking a specific project on?"

"Of course", she replied and he said he would get back to her. Within a week she had the role and her flight back to Canberra booked!

## Not Asking For What We Want Keeps Us Safe

Our comfort zone feels safe. It feels like we don't have to make any changes or rock the boat in any way. And that feels good because frankly it's part of the human condition to be wary of change. Quite frankly, the comfort zone feels safe because it *is* safe. But safe is not a good place to be when you're trying to build a business or a personal brand. And safe won't help you to put yourself out there to meet your goals and take on the world.

Nick Barnsdall, who I've mentioned earlier, and Joanne Brooks, who I've done a lot of work within the Queensland State Government, with the Ignite Project, both like to say, "*If you're not growing, you're dying*". If you play it safe, you'll never do anything more than what you're doing right now. And that is a recipe for becoming irrelevant and forgettable.

To grow, to aspire, to reach new heights you must, must step out of your comfort zone.

## Stepping Out of Your Comfort Zone

So, when was the last time you really stepped out of your comfort zone? Because unfortunately when you're building your personal brand this is the game. You'll probably be doing a lot of things that you've never done before, from building a website to putting yourself into your content, which means you're constantly in this space of getting comfortable with discomfort.

But if you don't do it, then what does that mean? Well, that means that you won't be setting up a website, or putting yourself in your content, or engaging with vulnerability – because those things simply aren't comfortable. Getting comfortable with discomfort is like going to the gym and discomfort is like a muscle. It's a matter of just using it every day, strengthening it so it becomes part of your normal routine.

I remember the first time I ever did a video blog. From memory it took about 35 takes before I got it right. First, I was terrible at getting the message across. Then the lighting looked wrong. Then I'd forgotten what I wanted to say. Then I noticed food in my teeth. Then my outfit looked a mess... it just seemed to go on and on. But after I (finally) got that first one off the ground, the second one became easier, and the third and fourth were easier still. I didn't necessarily get "better" at blogging - but I got better at letting go of perfectionism and accepting the discomfort that came from stepping out of my comfort zone and putting myself out there.

Interestingly, once I started to share with others that I felt so hopeless at it, they all said they'd faced the same challenges when they started. It just looked easy now after lots of practice. And as they reminded me – you just need to post the one that worked. No-one has to see all the ones that failed.

# When Fear Stops Driving You

When you've accepted the discomfort, then fear stops driving you and courage becomes your comfort zone. And the more you do it, the easier it will become. You'll soon find that putting yourself out there starts to feel, if not comfortable, then manageable. Eventually it will become your new comfort zone (and then you'll need to find another way to step out!).

At the end of the day you've got to keep getting clients into your business, connecting with your audience through your thought leadership, building networks and finding opportunities. To do that you have to constantly level up and get used to doing things (uncomfortable things) that you've never done before.

What will that be for you? Maybe it's time to increase your price or your salary. Maybe it's shifting from one-on-one clients to getting into a group workshop situation. Maybe it's time to chase that job. Maybe it's time to work with corporate clients. Maybe it's time to write your book!

Whatever it is, it's not going to happen from that comfort zone safe space. And it's time to step out from it.

## ❓ Key questions from here:

1. What is the thing that is out of your comfort zone that scares you a little bit (or maybe a lot), and that might be holding you back?

2. What strategies do you take to help you step outside of your comfort zone and get comfortable with discomfort? Think of when you have done this in the past.

3. Who is someone you know who has done this already?

4. What advice might they have for you?

5. If someone came to you for advice, what would you advise them to do?

6. List five things you could do in the next five days that would be uncomfortable. Put them in your calendar.

7. If you had to enroll a friend to help you achieve your goal or to hold you accountable, who might that be?

8. How will you measure your success?

9. What impact would it have for you to become better at this activity?

10. Measure your confidence muscle on a scale of one to 10 at the end of your five days. What have you noticed?

# CHAPTER 13

# Mind-Hack #10 –
# Be a Trailblazer

"Do not go where the path may
lead, go instead where there is
no path and leave a trail."

**– Ralph Waldo Emerson.**

Lillian Armfield was born on 3 December 1884 at Mittagong, New South Wales, daughter of George Armfield, a labourer, and his wife Elizabeth. Educated locally, she was highly intelligent, well-schooled and was described as having a good head for numbers.

In 1907 she became a nurse at the Hospital for the Insane, Callan Park, Sydney, where she looked after female inmates. Due to her competence and kindness to patients, in 1915, the medical superintendent recommended she apply for a newly established post. This post was as a police recruit in the NSW police force. At the time there were no female police officers in Australia, but this little hurdle didn't deter her. She thought she would be well suited to a career on the front line.

Lillian was successful in her application and in her starting role was paid the grand sum of 7 shillings, 6 pence a day. Unlike her male colleagues, however, Lillian's contract specified that no uniforms were to be provided and no overtime or expenses were to be allowed.

*Superintendent James Wilcox, Lillian Armfield*
*and Superintendent Gilbert Leary*

After a year's probation she was enrolled as a special constable, however, her promotion came with a catch. In what would seem unbelievable in today's workplace, Lillian was required to sign an agreement with the inspector-general of police. This made her subject to the same rules and discipline as her male colleagues. However, without the right to any compensation for injuries received in carrying out her duties. In addition to this overt discrimination, Lillian was also required to forego her right to superannuation and pension benefits upon retirement.

# Overseas interest

The experiment of Lillian Armfield's appointment was watched with intense interest overseas. She was the first plain-clothes female detective, exercising the same powers of arrest and working side-by-side with her male colleagues. So foreign was this concept of a female policewoman, that it gained international attention.

In Paris, a captain for the French police declared that policewomen would be the subject of jeers and prompted the following jingle in a Sydney newspaper:

*"In gay Paree no police you'll see*
*parading around in skirts*
*For France prefers her mademoiselles*
*as dainty, pretty flirts,*
*No Sergeant Armfield there you'll*
*find, forever on the roam,*
*The French would jeer at women cops.*
*They like their girls at home.*

*Oh ma Cherie, how sad 'twould be*
*if Suzannes or Suzettes*
*Discarded silks and chic coiffures*
*and scented cigarettes,*
*And turned to raiding restaurants*
*and tracking thief and crook.*
*No longer caring what the world*
*would wear or even cook"*

# The Trailblazer

Despite the ridicule, police from a number of American states asked for detailed reports of the experiment of women working as plain-clothed police officers. Scotland Yard rebuked any idea at the time of women working as plain-clothes detectives. However, they didn't rule out them working in uniform.

The forefront of Lillian's purpose was always to reclaim for society the women and girls who had turned to crime or had fallen into the wrong crowd. Much of her time was tracing runaway girls and encouraging them to return home before they encountered serious harm. It also often led her into cases involving murder, rape, theft, drug-running, prostitution—indeed the whole catalogue of crime.

Although her contribution was praised and officially recognised, promotion throughout her 34-year career was slow. By 1 November 1923, Lillian had become a special sergeant, 3rd class, and by 1 January 1943 had risen to 1st class. In 1947 she was awarded the King's Police and Fire Service Medal for outstanding service. After her retirement on 2 December 1949, aged 65, she was awarded the Imperial Service Medal in recognition of her contribution and service to the community.

*"She was a pioneer, a pathfinder for the present-day policewoman"*. The NSW Police Commissioner, Mr. N. T. W. Allan, said at her funeral.

## Her Influence

What makes this story so special and personal for me is that Lillian Armfield is my great Aunt. Her legend and trailblazing exploits as Australia's first policewoman is a story not lost in my own family. We are now made up of five members who are currently serving in various police roles across Australia.

Being one of three daughters, I can say that her story is something that has always inspired my sisters and me in our own careers. No matter what career path we've pursued, we've strived to always have the balance of kindness, courage to serve our clients and always have their interests at heart.

To be an influencer you don't have to be in *Time Magazine* or have thousands of followers on social media. In fact, it's not even about you. All that matters is who you influence and what impact you can make.

# Courageous Authenticity

Authenticity has been the content buzzword for the last year at least. I've written about it before and we often talk about it in my community. And everyone is in agreement – that when it comes to your personal brand or your practice, nobody wants just vanilla all the time, no matter how beautifully it's presented. Authenticity means embracing the things that make you uniquely you and protecting them at all costs. It's what makes you memorable and allows you to bring true value to the world.

All of that is still true. But now we need to do more. We need to embrace courageous authenticity.

## What is Courageous Authenticity?

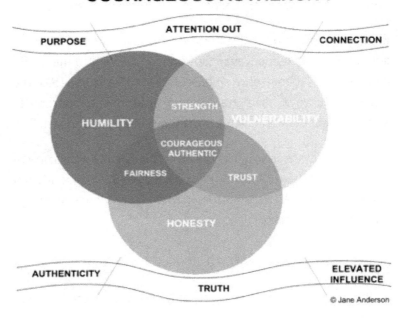

**COURAGEOUS AUTHENCITY**

© Jane Anderson

## Purpose + Attention Out + Connection

Courageous authenticity is essentially taking bold risks to help you achieve your big ticket goals. For Aunt Lillian this was putting herself into a dangerous, and predominantly male world, in order to help women find a better life. For each of us, it will be different. But in every case it involves the intersection of purpose, attention out and connection.

These attributes form the essence of how you can move past authenticity and into courageous authenticity. It's the connection of these attributes that have formed the purpose that drives you, connects you to your team or tribe and helps you turn your attention outward.

## Part 1: Vulnerability

Patrick Lencioni's best-selling book, *The Five Dysfunctions of a Team,* identifies the absence of trust as the first of the five dysfunctions.[36] He says that the absence of trust *"stems from their unwillingness to be vulnerable within the group".*[37] Because they aren't genuinely open with one another about their mistakes and weaknesses it becomes impossible to build a foundation for trust.[38]

When building courageous authenticity you start with vulnerability, but it's not simply being open. With courageous authenticity, it's about being open without ego.

This plays strongly into the idea of putting yourself out there. When I work with CEOs I often find them rabidly opposed to putting themselves into their organisation's social media. They say that they don't want to make it about them. But research shows that both staff and customers trust an organisation more when the CEO is active and open on social media.[39]

Getting to courageous authenticity means letting go of ego. So, for the CEOs, they need to recognise that putting themselves into social media, and being vulnerable while doing so, is not about them. It's about what's best for the organisation. We need to shift the language to how we're going to serve our clients, customers or organisation. Once ego is out of the picture, CEOs, and all other leaders and experts can truly use their vulnerability to help others.

## Part 2: Humility

When you're authentic, you're self-aware. But in courageous authenticity, it's not about you anymore. You've learned to be self-aware, and you've leaned into humility, and now it's time to go beyond and elevate those values. This is when you go into empathy.

When you have empathetic humility your attention is facing outward. You don't just understand intellectually what others are going through, but have a deep understanding that comes from recognising and even internalising the emotions of those going through those experiences.

## Part 3: Honesty

The last part of the model is about honesty. The more honest and straight you are with people, the more trust that you build. Elevating this honesty means that you're doing more than just scrupulously telling the truth. You're also being fair in all of your dealings with people – with your clients, your colleagues and your audience. Fairness is a courageous aspect of honesty.

Being scrupulously fair won't always win you friends. Certainly not those that want to be built up no matter what the situation calls for. But there are times when only straight-talking fairness will help someone move from being stuck, to being able to grow. It's vital in our businesses that we're able to do that. True helping means being fair and honest, always.

## The Intersections

What's important here is not so much the disparate parts of vulnerability, humility and honesty. What's important is what is created where these values intersect. You create trust where vulnerability and honesty intersect. You create fairness where honesty and humility intersect. And you create strength where humility and vulnerability intersect, strength.

It's these intersections that ultimately lead to elevating your authenticity to courageous authenticity.

### Taking Bold Risks

Courageous authenticity means taking bold risks. And it's this that can help you elevate your personal brand. When you put yourself out there you know you've got to be vulnerable, you know you have to be humble and you know you have to be authentic. You also know that you have to lean into discomfort by stepping out of your comfort zone. But taking bold risks is more than that.

Taking bold risks means trying the thing that no one else will try. It means speaking up when no one else will. It means struggling to the top of the heap of others doing the same thing that you're doing every day. Whatever those risks are, you need to be the one to embrace them if you want to be different, unique and brave. Innovation won't happen without risks. Progress won't happen without risks. And you will never learn if something might have worked if you don't take the risk and give it a go.

## Risks are Directly Related to Opportunities

Risks are directly related to opportunities, and isn't that why we're all here? Putting yourself out there is simply another way of saying grabbing opportunities. Your clients and customers have constantly changing demands. So you need to be in a constant state of progress. If you aren't innovating, responding and prioritising ways to bring new solutions to those demands then you will simply stop being relevant to your audience.

## ❓ Key questions from here:

1. What bold risk could you take in your business or career today?

2. What bold risk could you take in your business or career this week?

3. What bold risk could you take in your business or career this month?

4. What bold risk could you take in your business or career this year?

5. What bold risk could you take in your business or career in the next five years?

6. What does this mean for you and your career?

7. What's the worst that could happen?

8. What would you do if there was no plan B?

9. What would you do if you knew you couldn't fail?

10. Who are those around you that push you to take bold risks?

# IN CLOSING

This book covers a lot of ground from what putting ourselves out there really is, what holds us back and its implications for the future of work. The concepts in the book are designed to start the conversation and inspire you rather than make you feel overwhelmed. They're designed to help you consider how they may apply for you, your team and organisation as well as to consider what else builds your brand, trust, connection and influence for the people who matter in your world.

The ideas behind this book and the platform are designed to help give you a framework to consider, measure and gain insights into the areas where you have strengths and other areas that are an opportunity to focus on and improve. As each area improves there is a continuous levelling up that occurs whether it's each day, quarter or year as part of making more conscious and intentional choices around trust in building your tribe.

The key to remember is not to be afraid to start small. Whilst learning to put yourself out there may seem like a huge mountain to climb, it can just start with you taking a small step. One conversation, one idea at a time. Take the lead and be the example that others can follow. From there the ripple of change begins.

I would love to hear how you go implementing your mind-hacks. Please reach out to share your stories and examples to me at jane@jane-anderson.com.au.

I'm cheering you on!

# ENDNOTES

1.  Bita, N. (2014, January 17). GFC killed 250,000 Australian Jobs. News.com.au. https://www.news.com.au/finance/work/gfc-killed-250000-australian-jobs-news-story/6c2779af82bcb512e2843ee43f4f4cb2.

2.  Australian Bureau of Statistics. (2021). Weekly Payroll Jobs and Wages in Australia. https://www.abs.gov.au/statistics/labour/earnings-and-work-hours/weekly-payroll-jobs-andwages-australia/latest-release

3.  Wiseman, R. (2003). The Luck Factor. Individual and Organisational-Level Consequences of Organisation Citizenship behaviors: A Meta-Analysis. Skeptical Inquirer. http://richardwiseman.com/resources/The_Luck_Factor.pdf.

4.  Podsakoff, N., Whiting, S., Podsakoff, P., Blume, B. (2009) Individual and Organizational-Level Consequences of Organizational Citizenship Behaiors: A Meta-Analysis. Journal of Applied Behaviours: A Meta-Analysis.

5.  Ibid.

6.  Ibid.

7.  Clance, P. (2013). Imposter Syndrome. Paulineroseclance.com. https://www.paulineroseclance.com/impostor_phenomenon.html.

8.  Ibid.

9.  Mohr, T. (2014, August 25). Why Women Don't Apply for Jobs Unless They're 100% Qualified. Harvard Business Review. https://hbr.org/2014/08/why-women-dont-apply-for-jobs-unlesstheyre-100-qualified.

10. Ibid.

11. (2021, 25 January). The Confidence Gap in Men and Women: How to Overcome It. zengerfolkman.com. https://zengerfolkman.

12. Ibid.

13. Dweck, C. (2008). Mindset: The New Psychology of Success. Ballantine Books - Trade.

14. Ibid.

15. Enns, M.W., Cox, B.J. (2005). Perfectionism, Stressful Life Events, and the 1-Year Outcome of Depression. Cogn Ther Res 29, 541–553.

16. Handley, A.K., Egan, S.J., Kane, R.T. et al. (2014). The relationships between perfectionism, pathological worry and generalised anxiety disorder. BMC Psychiatry, 14, 98. https://doi.org/10.1186/1471-244X-14-98.

17. Cranab, A., Raja, B., Dharma, W. (2015). Perfectionism: A Risk to Self-Harm. i-manager's Journal on Educational Psychology, Vol. 8, No. 3, November 2014 - January 2015. https://files.eric.ed.gov/fulltext/EJ1098116.pdf.

18. Newby, J., Pitura, V., Penney, A., Klein, R., Flett, G., Hewitt, P. (2017). Neuroticism and perfectionism as predictors of social anxiety. Personality and Individual Differences, Volume 106. https://www.sciencedirect.com/science/article/pii/S0191886916310947.

19. Iketani, T., Kiriike, N., Stein, M., Nagao, K., Nagata, T., Minamikawa, N., Shidao, A. and Fukuhara, H. (2002). Relationship Between Perfectionism and Agoraphobia in Patients with Panic Disorder. Cognitive Behaviour Therapy, Volume 31.

20. Martinelli, M., Chasson, G., Wetterneck, C., Hart, J. and Björgvinsson, T. (2014). Perfectionism dimensions as predictors of symptom dimensions of obsessive-compulsive disorder. Bulletin of the Menninger Clinic. https://guilfordjournals.com/doi/10.1521/bumc.2014.78.2.140.

21. Bardone-Cone, A., Joiner, T., Crosby, R., Crow, S., Klein, M., le Grange, D., Mitchell, J., Peterson, C. and Wonderlich, S. (2008). Examining a psychosocial interactive model of binge eating and vomiting in women with bulimia nervosa and subthreshold bulimia nervosa. Behav Res Ther. 2008. https://pubmed.ncbi.nlm.nih.gov/18501334

22. Tyrka, A., Waldron, I., Brooks-Gunn, J. (2002). Prospective predictors of the onset of anorexic and bulimic syndromes. International Journal of Eating Disorders. https://pubmed.ncbi.nlm.nih.gov/12210642/

23. Rice, E., (2002). Risk and maintenance factors for eating pathology: a meta-analytic review. Psychology Buletin. https://pubmed.ncbi.nlm.nih.gov/12206196/.

24. Egan, S., Hattaway, M. and Kate, R. (2013). The Relationship between Perfectionism and Rumination in Post Traumatic. Stress Disorder. Cambridge University Press. https://www.cambridge.org/core/journals/behavioural-andcognitive-psychotherapy/article/abs/the-relationship-betweenperfectionism-and-rumination-in-post-traumatic-stress-disorder/8BCCD0AFD272B5AD0B92ED7085FC82EA.

25. Kempke, S., Van Houdenhove, B., Luyten, P., Goosens, L., Bekaert, P., Van Wambeke, P. (2011). Unraveling the role of perfectionism in chronic fatigue syndrome: Is there a distinction between adaptive and maladaptive perfectionism? Psychiatry Research. https://www.

26. sciencedirect.com/science/article/abs/pii/S0165178110005937.

27. Jansson-Fröjmark, M. and Linton, S. (2010). Is perfectionism related to pre-existing and future insomnia? A prospective study. British Journal of Clinical Psychology. https://bpspsychub.onlinelibrary.wiley.com/doi/full/10.1348/014466506X158824.

28. Dewey, D. (2004). Perfectionists' Appraisal of Daily Hassles and Chronic Headache. The Journal of Head and Face Pain. https://www.academia.edu/22227316/Perfectionists_Appraisal_of_Daily_Hassles_and_Chronic_Headache.

29. Fry, P., Debats, D. (2009). Perfectionism and the five-factor personality traits as predictors of mortality in older adults'. J Health Psychol. https://pubmed.ncbi.nlm.nih.gov/19383652/

30. Flett, G., Hewitt, P. (2014). The Destructiveness of Perfectionism Revisited: Implications for the Assessment of Suicide Risk and the Prevention of Suicide. Review of General Psychology. https://www.researchgate.netpublication277686664_The_Destructiveness_of_Perfectionism_Revisited_Implications_for_the_Assessment_of_Suicide_Risk_and_the_Prevention_of_Suicide.

31. Hill, A., Curran, T. (2015). Multidimensional Perfectionismand Burnout: A Meta-Analysis. Personality and Social Psychology

Review. https://www.researchgate.netpublication279191467_
Multidimensional_Perfectionism_and_Burnout_A_Meta-Analysis.

32. Ibid.

33. Brown, B. (2010, June). The Power of Vulnerability [Video]. Ted
Conferences. https://www.ted.com/talks/brene_brown_the_power_
of_vulnerability?language=en.

34. Ibid

35. Ibid

36. Carmichael, S. (Host). (2018, January 30). Women at Work: Make
Yourself Heard [Audio podcast episode]. HBR IdeaCast. Harvard
Business Review. https://hbr.org/podcast/2018/01/women-at-
workmake-yourself-heard.

37. Lencioni, P. (2011). The Five Dysfunctions of a Team: A Leadership
Fable. Jossey-Bass.

38. Ibid

39. Ibid

40. (2016). CEOs, Social Media, & Brand Reputation. Brandfog. https://
brandfog.com/BRANDfog2016CEOSocialMediaSurvey.pdf.

# WORK **WITH JANE**

In a world of constant change, there is a greater need for consultants and experts in their field to lead and help their clients navigate change. To do this they need a highly influential personal brand, catalyst content and effective business support to build their tribe.

With over 25 years experience and named as one of the top three branding experts in the world, Jane has helped over 100,000 people to build their identity and influence. She is a certified speaker, coach and has been featured on *Sky Business*, *The Today Show*, *The Age*, *Sydney Morning Herald*, *BBC* and *Management Today*. The author of six books, Jane typically speaks at conferences, runs workshops, consults and coaches and focuses especially on female leaders helping them to build their personal brand, thought leadership and sales.

Jane holds one of the top 1% viewed LinkedIn profiles and is the host of the *Jane Anderson Show* podcast where she has interviewed modern thinkers such as Seth Godin.

She has been nominated for and won over 10 marketing, business and coaching industry awards.

CORPORATE CLIENTS HAVE INCLUDED:

Telstra, International Rice Research Institute, Wesfarmers, Amadeus, Virgin Australia, IKEA, LEGO, Mercedes-Benz,

Australian Medical Association, Shell Energy and Workcover.

Book in a time to chat here:
https://calendly.com/jane-0877/complimentary-discussion
or
Email: support@jane-anderson.com.au
Call the office: +61 7 3841 7772

Alternatively jump on Jane's website at:
www.jane-anderson.com.au
to find out about her workshops, speaking and coaching programs.

# Read more of Jane's work

**By the end of 2021 the content marketing industry will have grown to a $412 billion dollar industry from just $156 billion in 2015.**

The rate of growth in content consumption has been dramatic and risk is that we start to create noise over signal.

In this book Jane talks about the power of thought leadership and how to put your ideas out there. She discusses the concepts of becoming prolific, creating the cadence of catalyst content that drives change.

This book is ideal for thought leaders, content creators and consultants looking to improve the quality and consistency of their thought leadership and content creation.

**Did you know your 40% more likely to achieve your goals if you write them down? That research led me to custom design this Personal Power Planner so it helps you stay aligned with your plan every day.**

Premium quality 100-page daily planner.

Designed to help you focus and stay aligned with your vision and goals – every day.

Simple, effective approach to managing time so you get your work done.

Includes a video guide on how to use your personal power planner to elevate your time management and achieve your goals.

**The old ways of growing a business have changed.**

Social media has levelled the playing field and now it's easier than ever to compete with the big players in your industry.

Whether you're a Thought Leader, Trusted Advisor, Academic or Expert, the way you position and market yourself is now more important than ever.

This book will help you uncover the 12 secret activities to grow your business and opportunities.

**Never has there been an opportunity for businesses and consultants to identify, engage and connect with their ideal audience like there is now with LinkedIn.**

By the end of this book, you will have the strategies you need to generate leads and grow your business using LinkedIn. You will be armed with practical steps that you can implement straight away to see real results. Your outcomes will be stronger, and you will lead the competition on this new playing field.

**In a world of disruption and constant change, we've become more transparent than ever. Organisations and their leaders at all levels are challenged with adapting to changing customer demands, leading growth and attracting and retaining great talent. They're being asked to be more transparent, authentic and credible than ever.**

In this sea of noise and trying to make sense of so much change, customers and employees connect with those who they trust.

In this book, Jane covers the 9 key skills of high trust brands and global influencers that lead with influence and communicate during change.

**We're no longer in the industrial or information age. We're now in the connection economy, where your ability to stand out, connect with others and position yourself in your career and business means security. It means you won't be left behind but instead be ahead of the pack.**

Companies and governments no longer want people who want jobs for life. They want innovation, ideas and networks to thrive in volatile economic times. We are bombarded with information and choices every day. Hard work alone doesn't cut it anymore.

Discover how to create "corporation you" without being a tall poppy to build your Personal Brand.

**We all hate selling ourselves, but interviews are one of those times when you can't be shy. You have to stand out from the crowd, and there's a way to give the panel what they want to hear without sounding like you're blowing your own trumpet.**

**From this book, you will learn** techniques to increase your confidence, how to anticipate the questions the panel might ask and how to practice in the lead-up to the big day.

CPSIA information can be obtained
at www.ICGtesting.com
Printed in the USA
LVHW010856240721
693546LV00010B/722